Agile: An Executive Guide

Real results from IT budgets

Second edition

Agile: An Executive Guide

Real results from IT budgets

Second edition

JAMIE LYNN COOKE

IT Governance Publishing
IT Governance Limited
Unit 3, Clive Court
Bartholomew's Walk
Cambridgeshire Business Park
Ely
Cambridgeshire
CB7 4EA
United Kingdom
www.itgovernance.co.uk

First published in the United Kingdom in 2011
by IT Governance Publishing.

ISBN 978-1-84928-189-8

Second edition published in 2016 by IT Governance Publishing.

ISBN: 978-1-84928-795-1

DEDICATION

To my sister, Susan, for being a constant inspiration in my life.

FOREWORD

Over the past two decades, Agile methods have enabled IT projects to deliver unprecedented levels of business value to organizations worldwide. Some of these benefits can be obvious from the first time that these approaches are used in an organization: higher quality outputs, more relevant software solutions, greater levels of user satisfaction, and tighter control of ongoing IT expenditure.

What may be less evident, however, are the compounded benefits that Agile methods can bring to organizations in the longer term: most notably, the establishment of an organizational culture that cultivates quality, inspires greater levels of employee motivation, and encourages staff to continually deliver high business-value outputs.

Agile: An Executive Guide gives you the bottom-line information that you need to harness the business-value benefits of Agile within your organization, and generate significantly greater returns on your IT investment.

Dr Jonathan Gray

Senior Researcher and Project Leader,
e-Government

National ICT Australia Limited (NICTA)

PREFACE

How often are the software development projects in your organization delivered on time? Within budget? Most importantly, how much is it costing you to *maintain* and *support* your delivered software to address usability issues, quality issues, or the inability of the delivered software to genuinely meet the current (and future) needs of the business?

It is no secret that information technology (IT) projects have earned a notorious reputation for budget overruns, missed deadlines, lack of alignment with the business, and dissatisfied users. These outcomes are so commonplace that they have become an expected part of the industry. (Just ask commercial software vendors how much they inflate their up-front development costs to allow for the inevitable overhead of addressing software problems during the warranty period?)

Arguably, the most quantifiable indicator of escalating software issues is the fact that, for many organizations, the 'support desk' has ballooned from a few part-time staff members to a fully staffed standalone department. This increase in the need for software support is not just due to the increasing number of IT systems and users; it is a symptom of software solutions which are being released with:

- fewer quality controls (bug fixes)
- less intuitive interfaces (phone and online support)
- a lack of alignment with the true business needs of the stakeholders (enhancements).

It does not matter whether your organization is a commercial software vendor, a 40-person IT consulting firm, or a large multinational with a dedicated IT department for internal business systems; whether you work in the private, not-for-profit or public sector; whether you are a recent start-up or an established company which has been in the industry for over 50 years. No organization is immune to these software issues. Which is exactly why Agile methods emerged in the first place.

Preface

Since the 1990s, Agile methods have provided the IT industry with an approach to software development that focuses on the quality, relevance and extensibility of software solutions. These approaches overcome traditional software development issues by positioning IT resources to regularly deliver *high business-value outcomes*; they replace up-front investment in software solutions with *incremental investment* based on proven business-value returns; most critically, they *protect the organization* from wasting money on software solutions that will only need to be reworked or replaced in the future because they do not meet the needs of the intended recipient.

In picking up this book, you have likely traded off your valuable time with one primary goal in mind – to decide whether Agile methods are worth pursuing in your organization – and, if so, to determine the best way to introduce, incorporate and leverage these approaches in your current environment.

Accordingly, this book has been written with only one objective: to provide IT executives and managers with the information that they need to make realistic (and justifiable) decisions on whether Agile is right for their organization, and the strategies to make it happen.

ABOUT THE AUTHOR

Jamie Lynn Cooke has 25 years of experience as a senior business analyst, project manager and solutions consultant, working with more than 130 public and private sector organizations throughout Australia, Canada and the United States.

She is the author of *Agile Productivity Unleashed: Proven Approaches for Achieving Real Productivity Gains in Any Organization*, a book written specifically to explain Agile methods in non-technical business terms to managers and executives outside of the IT industry; *Everything you want to know about Agile: How to get Agile results in a less-than-Agile organization*, which gives readers strategies for aligning Agile work within the reporting, budgeting, staffing, and governance constraints of their organization; and *The Power of the Agile Business Analyst: 30 surprising ways a business analyst can add value to your Agile development team*, which details 30 core activities that Agile business analysts can undertake to ensure that Agile development teams deliver the highest possible business value solutions for the organization.

She is also a well-regarded speaker on both business and technology topics, most recently presenting on issues such as: *Getting Management and Customer Support for Using Agile* and *When is Agile **Not** the Answer?* at the Business Process Modelling world conference in Brisbane, Australia and at the AgileCanberra professional forums.

Jamie has been working hands-on with Agile methods since 2003, and has researched hundreds of books and articles on Agile topics. She is a signatory to the Agile Manifesto, has attended numerous Agile seminars; and has worked with prominent consultants to promote Agile methods to numerous organizations worldwide.

Jamie has a Bachelor of Science in Engineering Psychology (Human Factors Engineering) from Tufts University in Medford, Massachusetts; and a Graduate Certificate in e-Business/Business Informatics from the University of Canberra in Australia.

ACKNOWLEDGEMENTS

My continued thanks to the pioneers and thought leaders of the Agile world, most notably Kent Beck, Martin Fowler, Alistair Cockburn, Jeff Sutherland, Mike Cohn, Ken Schwaber and Jim Highsmith, for their passionate work in developing and refining Agile methods over the past two decades.

Thanks also to the small and large organizations worldwide that have allowed their experiences in using Agile to be shared with others, including Nokia Siemens Networks™, Yahoo!™, Google™, Microsoft™ and BT™.

Special thanks to Vicki Utting and Angela Wilde of IT Governance Publishing, Neil Salkind of the Salkind Literary Agency, Stacey Czarnowski of Studio B and Liz Gill at LCI Proofreading & Editing Services for their ongoing support and sage advice.

Many thanks, as well, to the people who taught me the most about the strategies of the business world over the past 25 years, especially Roland Scornavacca, Tony Robey and Peter Walsh; to Rowan Bunning for being an unending source of Agile knowledge; to Dr. Jonathan Gray of NICTA for his industry insights; and to the writers and teachers who inspired me, particularly Richard Leonard[1] for his amazing ability to encourage writers with his humor and enthusiasm.

Finally, my eternal gratitude to my parents, my US family, my Australian family, and my friends, most especially Michele, Susan, Elissa, Janice and Linda, for continuing to be my sanity check in this world. Most of all, thank you to my husband, David, for 24 years of love and laughter.

[1] Richard Leonard's website: *www.richardleonard.net*.

CONTENTS

Chapter 1: An Executive Brief on Agile....1
What is Agile? 1
A two-minute history of Agile....3
The 10 core business benefits of Agile....7
Common Agile methods....8
Who uses Agile?....31
Chapter 2: What Can Agile Do For My Organization? ...33
Agile is not for every organization....33
Agile is not for every project....34
Dispelling Agile myths....35
Your Agile ROI....38
Your organizational culture....41
Your decision....44
Chapter 3: Five Steps to Agile Success....47
Step One: Choosing the right kick-off point....47
Step Two: Avoiding common traps....54
Step Three: Establishing your baseline....57
Step Four: Monitoring your investment....61
Step Five: Expanding Agile....65
More Information on Agile....69
ITG Resources....75

CHAPTER 1: AN EXECUTIVE BRIEF ON AGILE[2]

What is Agile?

'Agile' is a collective term for methods (and practices) that have emerged over the past two decades to increase the relevance, flexibility and business value of software solutions. These approaches are specifically intended to address the problems that have historically plagued software development activities in the IT industry, including budget overruns, missed deadlines, low quality outputs, and dissatisfied users.

> Agile methods are common-sense approaches for applying the finite resources of an organization to deliver high business-value software solutions.

Although there is a broad range of Agile methods in the IT industry – from software development and project delivery approaches to strategies for software maintenance – all of these methods share the same basic objectives:

- replace large up-front investment in software solutions with *incremental investment* based on business value returns
- focus project team members on delivering capabilities that generate the *highest business value* for the organization
- encourage *ongoing communication* between the business areas and project team members to increase the relevance, usability and quality of delivered software
- entrust and empower staff to *deliver value*
- position software solutions to be *responsive* to ongoing industry, organizational and technology changes.

---

[2] For those who follow this author's writing, some of the introductory material from *Agile Productivity Unleashed* and *Everything You Want to Know About Agile* has been adapted for use in this book, serving the same purpose as the original.

Some of the most common Agile methods include:

- iterative strategies for managing software development projects, such as *Scrum, Dynamic Systems Development Method (DSDM), Feature-Driven Development™ (FDD™),* the *Rational Unified Process® (RUP®),* and the *Agile Unified Process (AUP)*
- strategies for optimizing software development work, such as *eXtreme Programming (XP™)*, and *Lean Development*
- strategies for managing software development projects, as well as maintenance and support activities, such as *Kanban* and *Scrumban*
- extensions of Agile methods to support large enterprise-wide teams and shared corporate objectives, such as the *Scaled Agile Framework® (SAFe®), Scrum of Scrums, Large-Scale Scrum Framework (LeSS)* and *Nexus.*[3]

These Agile methods have been (and continue to be) successfully used by thousands of organizations worldwide[4], most notably in the United States, Europe and Australia. Some of the more prominent organizations using Agile methods include Nokia Siemens Networks™[5], Yahoo!™[6], Google™[7], Microsoft™[8], BT™[9], Bankwest™[10], SunCorp™[11], and Wells Fargo™[12].

---

[3] Further detail on these methods is provided in the Common Agile methods section of this chapter.

[4] As evidenced by the number of signatories to the Agile Manifesto (*www.agilemanifesto.org*) as at December 2015.

[5] NokiaSiemens and Agile Development, Haapio P, JAOO (2008): *http://jaoo.dk/file?path=/jaoo-aarhus-2008/slides//PetriHaapio_CanAGLobalCompany.pdf*.

[6] Lessons from a Yahoo! Scrum Rollout, Mackie K (2008): *http://campustechnology.com/articles/2008/02/lessons-from-a-yahoo-scrum-rollout.aspx*.

[7] Scrum Tuning: Lessons Learned at Google, Sutherland J (2006): https://www.youtube.com/watch?v=9y10Jvruc_Q.

[8] Microsoft Lauds Scrum Method for Software Projects, Taft D K (2005): *www.eweek.com/c/a/IT-Management/Microsoft-Lauds-Scrum-Method-for-Software-Projects/*.

In order to fully appreciate the effectiveness of Agile methods, it is worthwhile taking a couple of minutes to understand the business environment that caused these approaches to be established in the first place.

A two-minute history of Agile

In the 1990s, the IT industry was plagued by the remarkably high failure rate of software development projects; projects that became notorious for their missed deadlines, substantially overrun budgets, faulty deliverables and dissatisfied customers. A handful of thought leaders in the industry believed that these IT project failures could be attributed to three key factors: over-planning, insufficient communication and 'all-at-once' delivery.

Over-planning

IT software projects traditionally began with the production of extensive 'up-front' documentation, including project plans, functional requirements, system design specifications, and technical architectural designs. These documents, which often took months to produce (and even longer to get approved), were intended to ensure that the developed software would align with user requirements. In reality, however, these documents only served to provide corporate managers with a false sense of security in the expenditure of their IT budgets; and to ensure that delivered software would be substantially

---

[9] Agile Coaching in British Telecom, Meadows L and Hanly S (2006): *www.agilejournal.com/articles/columns/column-articles/144-agile-coaching-in-british-telecom*.

[10] Bankwest goes Agile: project time slashed, Braue D (2010): zdnet.com/bankwest-goes-Agile-project-time-slashed-1339306091/.

[11] Suncorp goes Agile for 19k desktop integration project (2008): itnews.com.au/News/130927,suncorp-goes-Agile-for-19k-desktop-integrationproject.aspx.

[12] Is Agile Development Only for Nerds?, Matta E (2008): *http://radiowalker.wordpress.com/2008/10/07/is-Agile-development-only-for-nerds/*.

misaligned with the ongoing – and changing – needs of the business.

The biggest problems with organizations relying upon up-front documentation were:

- the lack of responsiveness to ongoing changes in user requirements, market demand, internal resource availability and the capabilities of the underlying technologies
- the tendency for stakeholders (e.g. business areas, customers) to:
  - not clearly articulate their requirements (which were then left to the discretion of the technical team to interpret)
  - want everything under the sun (resulting in highly critical business requirements being lost in a sea of extraneous requirements)
- the inevitable misalignment between text descriptions of the users' needs and the resulting software.

The bottom line is that software products delivered to meet these up-front design documents were destined to fail – and businesses were losing millions in the process.

Insufficient communication

The second overwhelming driver in the ongoing failure of software development projects in the 1990s was the traditional – and often deliberate – separation of the business areas that required the software and the technical staff responsible for delivering the solution (i.e. development in a vacuum).

Once the big up-front design documents for an IT project were finalized, they were generally handed over to the technical team for development. The technical team was then sent back to their desks (often located in a separate section, floor or even building from the business areas) with a pile of paper and an immutable deadline. The next time that the technical team interacted with the business area was when they installed the resulting software on the users' machines for acceptance testing (or, even worse, production use).

This isolation created inevitable issues with the resulting software, including:

- user requirements left to the interpretation of the technical team members, without the benefit of understanding the business context
- the inevitable disconnect between the two-dimensional concept proposed in the documentation and the manifestation of that concept into tangible screens that the user could interact with
- not allowing for changes to business requirements that may have occurred between the time that the user was last consulted and the months (and sometimes years) that followed before the resulting software was installed on their system.

All of these factors resulted in the delivery of software that was frequently misaligned to the needs of the business users, including inadequate workflows, system errors, critical design flaws and features that were rarely (or never) used by the business – with no remaining budget or resources available to address these issues.

'All-at-once' delivery

Software development projects in the 1990s depended heavily on 'waterfall' project management methodologies, where analysis, design, development, testing and delivery stages were undertaken serially, requiring the full completion of one activity before the next one could begin. The use of waterfall methodologies on these projects meant that software design could not begin until all of the requirements analysis was complete; software testing could not begin until software development was complete; and software was not delivered to the users until all of the preceding stages had been completed.

This use of waterfall approaches in the IT industry was intended to reduce business risk in project delivery, requiring each step to be completed to management's satisfaction before further expenditure was incurred. In reality, waterfall approaches significantly increased the risk of IT project failure by:

- mandating big up-front documentation (with all of its related issues)
- discouraging responsiveness to changing requirements as the project evolved
- creating 'silos' of ownership that reduced communication across project team members.

Perhaps the most risky impact of these waterfall approaches, was delaying the delivery of tangible business outcomes until the very end of the project – when problems in the software are the most evident and changes to the software are the most costly.

Instead of enabling the organization to manage expenditures and risks throughout the software development project, executives were faced with an all-or-nothing proposition: keep pouring resources into a failing IT project, so that at least some value can be recovered from the previous investment, or end the project midstream and receive no tangible benefit to the organization. The 'all-at-once' delivery approach often left these executives with no other options.

There were, of course, other factors that influenced the high failure rate of software development projects in the 1990s, including limitations in technology and the lack of availability of skilled technical resources. However, the three issues outlined above – over-planning, insufficient communication and 'all-at-once' delivery – were factors that were *within the control of the organization to change*.

In order to combat the widespread failure of IT projects, a group of innovative thought leaders[13] began to develop strategies and practices that were specifically designed to address these three issues. It is their insight, along with the contribution of many others that followed, which has resulted

[13] Including Kent Beck, Martin Fowler, Alistair Cockburn, Jeff Sutherland and Ken Schwaber.

in the proven, business-value-driven Agile methods that are used throughout the world today.

The 10 core business benefits of Agile

The business value that Agile methods provide to organizations can be distilled into the following *10 core Agile business benefits*:

1. ***Ongoing risk management:*** by regularly confirming and adjusting requirements based on ongoing interaction with stakeholders; and by delivering fully functional and tested software features, so that technical risks are identified and mitigated throughout the process.
2. ***Ongoing control of budget expenditure:*** by providing decision makers with the opportunity to review and assess the business value of deliverables in each iteration, with the option to adjust, postpone or stop ongoing funding based on the return on investment (ROI) of delivered work.
3. ***Rapid delivery of tangible outcomes:*** by focusing team efforts on regularly producing fully functional and tested software features.
4. ***A focus on the highest-priority features:*** by continually working with key stakeholders to confirm and adjust the work undertaken by the project team to align with the most current priorities of the organization.
5. ***Strong alignment with business requirements:*** by directly involving key stakeholders in the initial and ongoing review of developed software, and by incorporating their feedback throughout the process.
6. ***Responsiveness to business change:*** by adjusting work throughout the process to incorporate organizational, industry and technology changes.
7. ***Transparency in status tracking:*** by regularly providing tangible outputs for stakeholder review, combined with open communication channels and centrally available status-tracking tools.
8. ***Substantially higher quality outputs:*** by incorporating rigid testing regimes throughout the software delivery process; and by working regularly with stakeholders to

confirm the usability and business value of delivered features.

9. ***Greater employee retention:*** by creating work environments that are based on high communication, empowering the team and trusting their expertise, encouraging innovation, and regularly acknowledging the team's contribution to the organization.[14]
10. ***Minimized whole-of-life software costs:*** by incorporating usability, quality and extensibility into software solutions throughout the delivery process, which reduces support and maintenance overheads; and by allowing additional functionality to be integrated into the solutions more cost effectively.

These combined benefits position organizations to receive a range of *real productivity gains*[15] from their software development activities. They enable these organizations to bring IT development work back under business control.

The following section provides an overview of some of the most common Agile methods, and identifies how each is designed to deliver these business benefits to your organization.

Common Agile methods

Figure 1, overleaf, summarizes the extent to which ten of the most common Agile methods deliver the *10 core Agile business benefits* identified in the previous section:

---

[14] From the team member's perspective, this collaborative and supportive work environment is arguably the most important business benefit of using Agile methods.

[15] See *www.realproductivitygains.com* for further detail on identifying and quantifying real productivity gains.

	Ongoing Risk Management	Ongoing Control of Budget Expenditure	Rapid Delivery of Tangible Outcomes	Focus on Highest-Priority Features	Strong Alignment with Business Requirements	Responsiveness to Business Change	Transparency in Status Tracking	Substantially Higher Quality Outputs	Greater Employee Retention	Minimised Whole-of-Life Software Costs
Scrum	✓	✓	✓	✓	✓	✓	✓	✓	✓	✓
Dynamic Systems Development Method (DSDM)	✓	✓	✓	✓	✓	✓	✓	✓	✓	✓
Feature-Driven Development™ (FDD™)	✓	✓	✓	✓	✓	Limited	✓	✓	✓	✓
Lean Development (Lean)	✓	✓	✓	✓	✓	✓	✓	✓	✓	✓
eXtreme Programming (XP™)	✓	Indirectly	✓	✓	✓	✓	✓	✓	✓	✓
Rational Unified Process® (RUP®)	✓	✓	✓	✓	✓	Limited	✓	✓	✓	✓
Agile Unified Process (AUP)	✓	✓	✓	✓	✓	Limited	✓	✓	✓	✓
Kanban	✓	✓	✓	✓	Limited	✓	✓	Limited	✓	✓
Scrumban	✓	✓	✓	✓	✓	✓	✓	✓	✓	✓
Scaled Agile Framework® (SAFe®)	✓	✓	✓	✓	✓	✓	✓	✓	✓	✓

Figure 1: Breakdown of the 10 core Agile business benefits by Agile method

Each of these methods is described in further detail in the following sections.

Scrum

Scrum is an iterative project management method most commonly used for Agile software development projects, but suitable for any project-based work. Scrum provides a framework for business areas to identify and prioritize work required, and for project teams to commit to the subset of priority items that they believe can be delivered in each two- to four-week iteration (or 'sprint').

> **Scrum** is an Agile method for project management that involves:
>
> - delivering software in time-boxed iterations
> - focusing on the highest business-value software features in each iteration
> - interacting directly with business users to confirm ongoing software usability, relevance and business value throughout the process.

Scrum requires the nomination of resources to provide key roles in the project, including:

- the *Product Owner* who represents the needs of the business, and is responsible for documenting and prioritizing solution requirements as input into ongoing planning
- the *Scrum Team*, a cross-disciplinary team charged with undertaking the agreed work in each sprint
- the *ScrumMaster* who facilitates the team's work, removing project impediments and ensuring that appropriate Scrum practices are being followed by the team.

Core to the success of Scrum are two activities that are undertaken for each iterative sprint:

- the *Sprint Planning Meeting*, held at the beginning of each sprint, where the Product Owner, ScrumMaster and Scrum Team review the highest-priority items identified by the

Product Owner and agree on the subset of priority items that will be included in the forthcoming sprint

- the *Sprint Review*, at the end of each sprint, which includes a demonstration of work completed in that sprint and a retrospective review of the work undertaken to enable continuous improvement for subsequent iterations.

Scrum also encourages teams to engage in *daily stand-up meetings*, short update sessions held each morning that enable the team to quickly review their completed and planned work and address any hurdles.

The progress of the Scrum Team's work is communicated to stakeholders through monitoring and measurement tools, such as:

- the *executive dashboard*, a report that summarizes the work within (and across) Agile teams for easy progress monitoring across the organization
- the *product backlog*, a reporting tool that enables both stakeholders and project teams to monitor the progress of work against the agreed business requirements[16]
- the *sprint backlog*, a reporting tool that enables teams to monitor and manage their actual day-to-day work.

Scrum is arguably the most commonly used Agile approach worldwide, and a range of professional courses are available to certify people for roles such as the ScrumMaster and Product Owner. These courses foster the consistent and effective application of these roles in every organization. They are also intended to address common areas of misapplication in Scrum implementations, such the mistaken view of the ScrumMaster as a project manager (instead of a facilitator).

This collaborative approach to project management and status tracking – combined with regular reviews of tangible outcomes and business-driven prioritization of ongoing work – positions Scrum to deliver all of the *10 core business benefits of Agile*.

---

[16] Some Scrum teams also use a Release Backlog to identify and manage subsets of capabilities that are planned for delivery in scheduled releases.

Dynamic Systems Development Method

The Dynamic Systems Development Method (DSDM) framework is another iterative approach to managing Agile software development projects. It has its roots in Rapid Application Development (RAD), resulting in a strong emphasis on building prototypes and confirming the feasibility of the solution with the business prior to undertaking full development activities. This is evidenced by DSDM requiring Stakeholder Workshops, a Feasibility Report, a Feasibility Prototype and a Business Study to be undertaken prior to full implementation.

> **Dynamic Systems Development Method (DSDM)** is an Agile method for project delivery that involves:
>
> - delivering software in time-boxed iterations
> - prototyping and documenting the software solution prior to undertaking full development activities
> - collaborating with users, producing tangible outputs, and ensuring quality management throughout the process.

The practices that underpin DSDM are at the very heart of Agile methods, including active user involvement throughout the process, iterative and incremental development, frequent delivery of tangible outputs and empowering the team. Ongoing testing and quality control of software throughout the process are also emphasized. These practices combine to enable DSDM, like Scrum, to deliver all of the *10 core business benefits of Agile*.

Unlike Scrum, however, the DSDM framework requires a range of artifacts (e.g. development plans, functional models) to be developed at each phase of the project to provide ongoing confirmation that planned work is aligned with the needs of the business.

Although the approaches differ, both Scrum and DSDM have the same core objective – the delivery of high business-value outcomes in controlled, iterative timeframes. Scrum provides a high-level framework for achieving this objective, and relies on communication between the participants to ensure that work undertaken meets ongoing business needs. DSDM provides a more structured framework to achieve this objective, requiring proposed work to be documented and confirmed prior to continuing to the next stage.

Feature-Driven Development™

Feature-Driven Development (FDD™) is an Agile method that combines elements of iterative project management with practices that are specific to software development. The basic driver of FDD™ is providing incremental value to the business by delivering complete, working product capabilities (i.e. software 'features' and 'feature sets') in every iteration.

> **Feature-Driven Development (FDD™)** is an Agile method that combines iterative project delivery with software development practices by:
>
> - having teams model the business problem up front
> - decomposing the model into smaller features and feature sets
> - integrating selected feature sets into the overall software solution through iterative releases
> - keeping a strong focus on collaboration with users, production of tangible outputs, and quality management throughout the process.

FDD™ requires close collaboration with the business areas to establish an up-front 'domain model' of the business problem that the proposed system is intended to address. Once this domain model is identified, it is broken down (decomposed) into smaller units (i.e. 'features') that are able to be developed and delivered iteratively. Team members are then assigned to build nominated features which, once successfully tested, are incorporated into the larger system.

In many respects, FDD™ works from the same underlying principles as other Agile methods (e.g. Scrum), in that the project team works closely with the business areas to deliver regular, incremental value to the organization. However, FDD™ is far more prescriptive about defining the boundaries of the solution up front, assigning specific roles and responsibilities to the team members, and controlling the scope of each team member's work during the actual software development process.

Based on the above, there is an argument to say that, although FDD™ delivers all *10 core business benefits of Agile*, its ability to deliver 'responsiveness to business change' is limited. This is because the structure of FDD™ makes it less responsive to ongoing organizational, industry or technology changes that do not fit in with the originally identified domain model.

Lean development

Lean development (Lean) is an Agile method that combines elements of iterative project management with best practices in software design and development. Lean stems from the Lean manufacturing processes that originated as early as 1922[17], but most closely aligns with the principles of Kaizen[18] and Total Quality Management (TQM)[19].

At the heart of Lean is *value stream mapping*, focusing on:

- identifying and confirming the business value of customer requirements
- delivering the highest business-value software features
- making software development processes as *efficient* as possible.

As a corollary to this, Lean promotes the identification and elimination of *areas of waste*

> **Lean Development (Lean)** is an Agile method that combines elements of iterative project management with best practices in software design and development by:
>
> - using *value stream mapping* to deliver the highest business-value features within the most efficient software development process
> - incorporating *pull techniques* and *optimal capacity planning* to deliver results as quickly as possible
> - enforcing stringent quality management through integrity checking and continuous improvement
> - empowering skilled cross-functional teams to deliver the highest value outcomes to the organization.

---

[17] *My Life and Work*, Ford H with Crowther S, Garden City Publishing Company, Inc. (1922), ISBN 9781406500189.

[18] *KAIZEN - The Japanese Strategy for Continuous Improvement*, Kotelnikov V www.1000ventures.com/business_guide/mgmt_kaizen_main.html.

[19] *TQM. Total Quality Management. An Integrated Approach to Quality and Continuous Improvement*, Kotelnikov V www.1000ventures.com/business_guide/im_tqm_main.html.

within the software development process (e.g. project teams unable to progress their work because they are waiting on input from the business).

Another core principle of Lean is *fast delivery* (deriving from queueing theory and just-in-time practices), which encourages teams to:

- use *pull* techniques to respond to customer needs as they emerge
- align the volume and complexity of their work with their optimal capacity to deliver.

In support of this, Lean encourages the team to hold off on making decisions as long as reasonably possible in the software development process, to provide maximum flexibility in addressing ongoing business requirements.

Lean also incorporates stringent quality management techniques by enforcing system integrity at both the business requirements and technical levels, by promoting system optimization and software testing throughout the process, and by encouraging the team to regularly review and critique their work for continuous improvement.

In addition to optimizing the software development process, Lean focuses on the critical importance of having a cross-functional project team which is sufficiently skilled, resourced and empowered to continually deliver the highest value outcomes to the organization.

It is the combination of these factors that enables Lean to deliver all of the *10 core business benefits of Agile*.

eXtreme Programming (XP™)

eXtreme Programming (XP™) is an activity-specific Agile method for iterative software development work. XP™ encourages software developers to produce and deliver the *simplest possible technical solution* required to meet the customer's objectives; *anticipates that requirements will change* once the customer has had an opportunity to work with the delivered software; and encourages the *ongoing improvement and optimization* of the software based on customer feedback.

> **eXtreme Programming (XP™)** is an Agile method for software development work that is based on:
>
> - delivering the simplest possible technical solution required to meet the customer's objectives
> - anticipating that requirements will change once the customer has had an opportunity to work with the delivered software
> - encouraging the ongoing improvement and optimization of the software based on customer feedback.

Unlike the 'big up-front documentation' approaches that burdened the IT industry in the 1990s, XP™ documents business requirements at a high level – and then works *hands-on* with the customer to deliver their desired outcomes using the simplest designs, delivered in the earliest possible timeframes.

XP™ incorporates the use of an Agile practice called *Test-Driven Development (TDD)*, which encourages software developers to create the tests that will be used to validate the code that they are building *prior to* undertaking development work. TDD is an innovative quality management approach, requiring team members to define and document their measures of success prior to undertaking the work required.

Another Agile practice used in XP™ is a concept known as *refactoring*, which allows the team to regularly review the existing system and modify it, where required, so that future software changes can be implemented more easily. Amazingly, this includes full authority for the team to *throw away* existing software in favor of a replacement solution that will provide the organization with greater flexibility to address future requirements. XP™ advocates that the short-term loss of work undertaken is worth the long-term opportunity for software solutions to grow with the organization more cost-effectively.

XP™ also utilizes a number of other Agile practices that enable its practitioners to regularly deliver high-quality output and reduce ongoing maintenance costs, including pair programming (having two members of the delivery team work together on assigned tasks to increase accountability and knowledge sharing), automated testing and continuous integration.[20]

The iterative and customer-driven nature of XP™ enables it to deliver all of the *10 core business benefits of Agile*; however, as XP™ is not a formal project management methodology[21], its ability to influence ongoing budget management with decision makers is only able to be achieved indirectly through customer feedback (or in combination with other Agile methods, such as Scrum).

It is the simplicity of design, the expectation of change, and the freedom provided to the team to rethink and optimize software solutions that make XP™ one of the most well-regarded and widely used Agile methods.

Rational Unified Process®

The Rational Unified Process® (RUP®) is a framework of Agile best-practice approaches that are designed around iterative software development work, with a strong focus on *identifying and addressing risks* as early in the project as possible. Although the framework is flexible to adapt to the

---

[20] XP™ is better suited to technology platforms that support practices such as refactoring and continuous integration. Older and more restrictive systems may not be viable platforms for these practices.
[21] Noting that there is an emerging interest in using the powerful techniques of XP for eXtreme Project Management

needs of each project, the primary objective of risk mitigation is a critical factor in every RUP® implementation.

RUP® work is commonly divided into four phases:

1. **Inception:** This is when the project scope is identified and confirmed through a business case, a description of the work, an initial (or basic) use case model, budget forecasting, an estimated delivery schedule, and a risk assessment. All aspects of the planned project work are confirmed by key stakeholders prior to progressing to the next phase.
2. **Elaboration:** This is when the team develops the bulk of the use cases (which document the users' interaction with the system) and the system architecture for the solution. The primary focus of this phase is the identification and mitigation of technical risks in the solution. This is done by adding in use cases that specifically target identified risks, prototyping risk areas to show that they can be addressed, and by utilizing an executable architecture for the most critical use cases. Work within this phase can be done iteratively, with the most risky areas being addressed in the initial iterations. Original project estimations are confirmed during this phase, which includes the creation of a detailed development plan for stakeholder confirmation. The elaboration phase is considered complete when stakeholders are confident that all identified risks have been sufficiently addressed, that the system design is sound, and that the updated project schedule (including budget utilization and resourcing) is sufficiently accurate to proceed.
3. **Construction:** This is when the actual development work is undertaken by the team in support of the approved use cases. The RUP® is not prescriptive about the development platform that teams use, but strongly advocates the use of an object-oriented environment to facilitate the development and integration of discrete use cases, which then provides a greater opportunity for ongoing quality control and code reuse. Work in the construction phase is generally done across multiple iterations, culminating with an initial

operational capability (IOC) review, where stakeholders assess developed capabilities and confirm project readiness for deployment.

4. **Transition:** This is when the approved capabilities are deployed to users with the necessary documentation and training to support the successful use of the solution in a production environment. Depending on the size of the system, work in the transition phase can also be done iteratively, with subsets of capabilities released when the organization is in a position to utilize them. Transition phase work continues until the users are able to utilize – and are satisfied with – all the released capabilities (i.e. the 'product release milestone').

A key differentiation between the RUP® and other Agile methods (e.g. Scrum) is that, with the RUP®, the iterative work of the elaboration, construction and transition phases is done *within the boundaries of the initial scoping work* that was done in the inception phase. Accordingly, the RUP® is considered to be an *iterative software development method*, instead of an iterative project delivery method. The result is that the RUP® can be used to mitigate the risks associated with implementing agreed functionality, but is less effective at addressing the risks of internal or external changes to business requirements as project work progresses.

For organizations transitioning from waterfall to Agile approaches in software development, the RUP® can provide a 'safer' starting point: one that introduces the project team to the principles and practices of iterative work without dramatically changing the upfront specification approach that they are familiar with. Similarly, for projects that are subject to existing scope constraints (e.g. fixed scope contracts), the RUP® offers a way to introduce some of the key benefits of Agile (primarily risk mitigation) within the immovable constraints of a fixed deliverable. It is, however, important to recognize the limitations of the RUP® in delivering all of the *10 core business benefits of Agile*. Like FDD™, the RUP® framework has limited 'responsiveness to business change' because all of the project work is done within the boundaries of the initial scoping work that was done in the inception phase.

> The **Rational Unified Process (RUP®)** is an iterative Agile software development method that focuses on identifying and addressing risks as early in the project as possible.
>
> The RUP® is executed through four phases: inception, elaboration, construction and transition. The initial scope and metrics for the project (e.g. timeline, budget) are identified in the inception phase. Iterative work can be undertaken over the next three phases, but always within the constraints of the initially approved project scope.
>
> Risk management is a critical component of all four phases of the RUP®, with progression to each subsequent phase contingent upon the successful demonstration that identified risks have been sufficiently addressed.

Agile Unified Process

For organizations that want the discipline of the RUP® and the benefits of XP™ practices, the Agile Unified Process (AUP) provides a 'best of all worlds' Agile approach.

The AUP works within the inception, elaboration, construction and transition phases of the RUP®, but simplifies the structure of the RUP® to seven key disciplines: *model, implementation, test, deployment, configuration management, project management* and *environment*. Importantly, the AUP incorporates numerous Agile practices (particularly XP™ practices) as part of the iterative work *within* the RUP® phases to ensure that development is continually focused on delivering the customer's highest-priority features as an extensible, elegant, user-driven solution. To further supplement the risk management features of RUP®, the AUP advocates migrating iterative releases of tested functionality into a *pre-production* environment prior to the full transition of the solution into the live environment.

> The **Agile Unified Process (AUP)** provides a 'best of all worlds' Agile method, particularly for organizations who want the benefits of Agile within a more stringent risk management structure.
>
> Combining the RUP® and the best practices of XP™, the AUP gives organizations the artifacts that they expect from a traditional software development process, but equally delivers most of the core benefits of Agile with the iterative delivery of the customer's highest-priority capabilities.

As described by its creator, Scott Ambler, the AUP is 'serial in the large' and 'iterative in the small'[22].

The AUP provides *lightweight documentation*, with teams having the option to refer to more detailed guidelines as needed. The AUP is also *adaptable*, so that teams can apply those practices that are best suited to the needs of each project.

To facilitate the adaptation of the developed solution to meet ongoing business requirements, the AUP further encourages teams to use simple tools, scalable architectures and database refactoring.

In many respects, the AUP is the ideal approach for more traditional organizations that are transitioning to Agile methods, as it combines both the core principles of Agile and the power of XP™ practices with the risk management

---

[22] The Agile Unified Process (AUP): www.ambysoft.com/unifiedprocess/agileUP.html

structure of the RUP® and the standard artifacts that organizations expect from a traditional software development process. It does, however, have similar limitations as the RUP® in delivering all of the *10 core business benefits of Agile*, specifically in 'responsiveness to business change' due to the constraints established in the inception phase.

Kanban

Kanban is an Agile workload management and change management method that can be used in conjunction with or independently from other Agile methods. It is often used to manage IT support and maintenance activities, where priority work can change on a weekly, daily or even hourly basis.

> **Kanban** is an Agile method for workload management that is used to:
>
> - allow teams (including IT support and maintenance teams) to manage their workload in order to
>   - ensure optimal throughput
>   - accommodate changing requirements
> - make ongoing work transparent to all stakeholders to encourage communication, collaboration and problem solving.
>
> Kanban is able to be used in conjunction with other Agile methods (e.g. Scrum) to allow the team to integrate their flow-based work into project frameworks.

At the heart of Kanban, is empowering the project team to regularly deliver business value by employing *lean practices* to make their work as efficient and manageable as possible. One of the primary methods for achieving this is by limiting the team's work in progress (WIP) at any point in time, enabling them to *maintain their focus* on completing the highest priority work. This approach enables the team to focus on completing a fixed number of tasks that are optimized for their capacity to deliver to quality standards: no more and no less. If the business requires a higher priority task to be addressed, stakeholders and team members must determine what current work should be postponed in order to free up sufficient resources to address the requirement. Equally, if the team has an opening in the WIP queue, they can *pull in* the next highest priority work identified by the stakeholders.

Kanban uses the practice of *visualizing the workflow* through the use of centralized *Kanban boards* to make the following information evident to all stakeholders at any time:

- the status of all of the team's planned, current and completed work
- the team's availability to take on additional work
- any hurdles that are preventing work from progressing.

Not only does this practice create an environment of open communication, transparency and collaboration; it promotes a culture of continuous improvement by encouraging teams to address bottlenecks, overcome hurdles, and maximize their productivity throughout the process.[23]

Where Scrum prescribes managing work by time-boxed iterations, and FDD™ prescribes committing to work by deliverable features, Kanban is far less prescriptive on *how* a body of work is defined, or *when* it can be delivered. Instead, Kanban allows the team to establish review cycles and release timeframes based on the specific requirements of the organization. To accommodate this, Agile practitioners have begun using hybrid methods, such as Scrumban (a combination of Scrum and Kanban) to incorporate effective Agile practices, such as retrospectives, into the optimized workflows of Kanban. (Details on Scrumban are provided in the next section.)

It is important to note that Kanban is a method for managing what work is being done by the team, and for allowing the

[23] Some organizations choose to manage all of the work across a department on one Kanban board, with colored sticky notes used to distinguish separate initiatives. This enables commitments and resource availability across the department to be viewed more holistically.

organization to continually *adjust* the tasks on the Kanban board to address the highest priority business requirements. Unlike other Agile methods, however, Kanban *does not* prescribe how the team works with stakeholders to identify and confirm software features, nor does it prescribe how these features are tested and integrated into existing software components. Accordingly, Kanban delivers most of the *10 core business benefits of Agile*, with 'strong alignment with business requirements' and 'substantially higher quality outputs' only delivered to a limited extent.

Scrumban

In describing the range of Agile methods above, it was identified that most Agile approaches are designed to deliver efficiencies within *a specific area of focus*, such as iterative project management or iterative software development. In response to this, many organizations have chosen to implement *hybrid* or *custom* Agile approaches, which leverage the benefits across several different Agile methods.

One of the most commonly combined Agile methods is Scrum (as an overarching project management approach), which can be used in conjunction with more targeted software development methods (e.g. XP™ or Lean). In particular, there is significant use of the combined Scrum and Kanban methods (known as *Scrumban*) to integrate the flow management, visualization and lean principles of Kanban with the structure and practices of Scrum work.

The interesting thing about Scrumban is that it can be perceived (and implemented) in two distinctly different ways.

The first approach for implementing Scrumban is where teams apply Kanban capacity workflow management and lean practices *within* the Scrum project management framework. In this approach:

- the prioritized product backlog feeds the 'to do' column in the team's Kanban board with the aim of maintaining an optimal number of product backlog items in the queue at all times to ensure the ongoing availability of high-priority work

- the team manages their capacity (and focus) by controlling the number of product backlog items that are actively being worked on (their 'Work in Progress') and by 'pulling in' new work when they have availability[24]
- all of the columns on the Kanban board have defined minimum and maximum limits, where exceeding these limits (in either direction) triggers actions to be taken to ensure continuous workflow
- standard Scrum practices (e.g. daily stand-ups, retrospectives) and Scrum roles (e.g. Product Owner, Scrummaster) are used, however:
    - teams are less focused on the upfront estimates and commitments that are typically used in sprint planning, and more focused on ensuring that product backlog items are small and achievable to maintain consistency in their throughput cadence
    - sprint retrospectives focus more on establishing lean process efficiencies to *decrease the cycle time* for each product backlog item (i.e., the time required to get each item through the flow and ready for release) than on the detailed analysis of velocity or confirming the accuracy of previous estimates.

In addition to flow management efficiencies, Scrumban focuses the team on *visualizing the complete user story* as they do their work, not just the subset of features in the current sprint backlog.

The second way of implementing Scrumban is more holistic, where focusing on the highest priority work carries up through the enterprise as a *continuous process*, not restricted by sprint structures or milestones. In this 'prioritization on demand'

---

[24] In Scrumban, when team members have completed a WIP task, they will first focus on what is needed to help other team members complete their WIP tasks before pulling in new work (known as 'swarming' to address the highest priority WIP tasks for the team overall). This can include taking on different roles (e.g. testing) to provide whatever assistance is needed to complete the task.

approach, the business feeds requirements into the backlog (and, subsequently, the 'to do' column of the Kanban board) *as they become known* - and then re-prioritizes them as often as needed to support emergent information. This means that Product Owners do not need to wait for a formal sprint planning session to have their new (or newly prioritized) requirements added to the team's 'to do' column - requirements can be updated and reprioritized as part of a continuous flow. This is what the author of the first materials on Scrumban[25], Corey Ladas, intended when he described it as a way of using Kanban to deliver lean software development *across the enterprise*.

Both approaches to Scrumban deliver the *10 core business benefits of Agile*, although there is an argument to say that the second, more holistic, approach delivers greater responsiveness to business change overall.

Scrumban is a hybrid Agile method for delivering high business-value outputs based on team capacity, with a continuous focus on optimizing throughput. It can be implemented either as:

- a Kanban workflow management model within the Scrum project management framework, or
- a more holistic method for the continuous delivery of high-priority work across the enterprise.

[25] Scrumban - Essays on Kanban Systems for Lean Software Development, Corey Ladas, 2009 Modus Cooperandi Press

Scaled Agile Framework® (SAFe®)[26]

The Agile methods described in this section have focused primarily on *team level* project delivery, i.e., practices that are suitable for an individual small- to medium-sized development team. In larger IT departments with hundreds of developers, the organization may want to consider scaling these methods to enable the coordination of larger groups of resources towards shared objectives. This expansion is generally achieved by either:

- Scaling up the work that is done by an individual Agile team (particularly Scrum teams) to support the equivalent work across multiple teams - with aggregated artifacts (e.g. a shared product backlog across teams) and scaled communication channels. Examples of this type of approach include *Scrum of Scrums*, the *Large Scale Scrum (LeSS)* framework and *Nexus*[27]
- Coordinating and driving Agile work at *portfolio, program* and *project* levels to synchronize the work across multiple Agile teams to align with shared corporate objectives. One of the most widely known and used approaches to achieve this is the Scaled Agile Framework® (SAFe®).

SAFe® provides a structure for integrating Agile work across the enterprise by identifying specific processes and roles for:

- managing the delivery of required outcomes through Value Streams (portfolio level), Program Increments and Releases (program level) and Iterations (team level)
- managing business requirements as Epics and Program Epics (across releases), Features (within releases) and User Stories (within iterations)
- managing the system architecture to ensure consistency and efficiency in system design at all levels, including an 'intentional architecture runway' to support planned work.

The SAFe® integrated framework provides:

---

[26] Designed by Dean Leffingwell and Scaled Agile, Inc.

[27] The More Information on Agile section provides links to detailed information on these methods.

a single, unified view of the work to executives, allowing them to drill down for details or up for trends and analysis[28]

allowing Agile work to be managed and monitored at every level of the enterprise.

To maintain the productivity and integrity of Agile methods, SAFe® also ensures that the core Agile practices of iterative work, test driven development, continuous integration and refactoring are undertaken at the team level, as well as providing overarching architectural governance and synchronization at the higher levels.

The official SAFe® website at *www.scaledagileframework.com* provides a complete picture of the framework, including detail on the processes, roles and outputs at each level.

As SAFe® supports Agile methods at the enterprise level, it is positioned to deliver all of the *10 core business benefits of Agile* and, in many respects, can achieve this more broadly than Agile work that is used exclusively at the team level.

> The **Scaled Agile Framework® (SAFe®)** is a method for delivering enterprise level Agile work to achieve integrated portfolio, program and project objectives across the organization.
>
> SAFe® allows organizations with hundreds of developers to synchronize their work using Agile methods to ensure the ongoing business value, consistency and integrity of their delivered outputs.

[28] Introducing the scaled agile framework: *www.cio.com/article/2936942/enterprise-software/introducing-the-scaled-agile-framework.html*

It is important to note that the descriptions in this section represent only ten of the Agile methods available to your organization. There are several other Agile methods in use (and emerging) throughout the IT industry, including *Disciplined Agile Delivery (DAD)* and *Crystal*. The More Information on Agile section at the end of this book provides you with links to industry resources on additional Agile methods for your consideration.

It may also be worthwhile reviewing an excellent comparison matrix provided by DevX at: *www.devx.com/architect/Article/32836/0/page/4*, which provides further detail about several of the Agile methods described above.

Who uses Agile?

As identified at the start of this chapter, Agile methods are used by thousands of organizations worldwide, including Nokia Siemens Networks™, Yahoo!™, Google™, Microsoft™ and BT™, to produce high business-value outcomes in the delivery of their software solutions. They have been equally successful in private and public sector organizations of all sizes, particularly throughout the United States, Europe and Australia.

As an example, one of the most common Agile methods, Scrum, is used by prominent organizations worldwide, including Adobe™, Barclays Global Investors™, BBC™'s New Media Division, BellSouth™, Bose™, CapitalOne™, Federal Reserve Bank™, GE™, Google™, Microsoft™, Motorola™, Nokia Siemens Networks™, SAP™, State Farm™ and Yahoo!™[29]

[29] The use of Scrum by these organizations is documented in a number of sources, including corporate websites, industry publications (e.g. *Microsoft Lauds Scrum Method for Software Projects*, Taft DK (2005): *www.eweek.com/c/a/IT-Management/Microsoft-Lauds-Scrum-Method-for-Software-Projects/*), the work undertaken by industry experts such as Jeff Sutherland (*www.scrumalliance.org/community/profile/jsutherland*) and case

A recent survey undertaken by VersionOne™ indicates that organizations that use Agile in their software delivery are achieving increased productivity (84% of respondents), faster time to market (77% of respondents) and improved ability to manage changes in priorities (87% of respondents).[30]

This track record can give readers confidence in knowing that Agile methods are sustainable, proven approaches that are successfully used throughout the global marketplace. For executives, however, the most critical question is often: What can Agile do for ***my*** organization?

---

studies at industry events, e.g. *The Growth of an Agile Coach Community at a Fortune 200 Company*, Silva K & Doss C, AGILE 2007 (13-17 Aug 2007), Washington DC: *http://ieeexplore.ieee.org/Xplore/login.jsp?url=http%3A%2F%2Fieeexplore.ieee.org%2Fiel5%2F4293562%2F4293563%2F04293600.pdf%3Farnumber%3D4293600&authDecision=-203*.

[30] 9th Annual State of Agile Development Survey: *http://info.versionone.com/state-of-agile-development-survey-ninth.html*.

CHAPTER 2: WHAT CAN AGILE DO FOR MY ORGANIZATION?

Before we identify the many things that Agile methods can do for your organization, it is important to identify the types of organizations and projects that are best suited for Agile work and to clear up some common misconceptions surrounding these methods.

Agile is not for every organization

Agile methods are extremely effective at addressing two of the most common challenges in software delivery:

- responsiveness to change, and
- the sustainable production of high business-value outputs within project constraints.

This means that, the more that your organization is faced with ongoing changes to requirements and/or unsustainable IT overheads, the better positioned you are to receive substantial returns on your Agile investment.

The ROI value that your organization is likely to receive from utilizing Agile methods is directly correlated to the following risk factors:

- your organization's level of exposure to ***external change***, including changes in customer requirements, fluctuations in market demand, announcements from competitors, and the availability of new technologies
- your organization's level of exposure to ***internal change***, including changes in user requirements, technology platforms, staff departures, business priority shifts, and funding reallocations
- the sustainability of your ***current IT overheads***, including:
    - the ability to deliver software solutions within agreed timelines and/or budgets
    - the quality of delivered solutions and the cost of rework, support and maintenance

  - the ability for delivered solutions to adequately support current and future business requirements
  - high turnover rates (or low productivity levels) in your IT departments.

For organizations with *highly predictable* and *replicable* business processes - and organizations where software solutions are generally delivered *on time* and *on budget*, *meet business requirements* and require *minimal ongoing support* to address quality and usability issues - Agile methods can provide some degree of benefit to the organization, but not the dramatic benefits that organizations with more dynamic (and less sustainable) software solutions can achieve.[31]

Agile is not for every project

In the same way that the benefits of using Agile methods will vary across organizations, they will also vary across project types. You are more likely to deliver a successful Agile project in an environment where:

- management supports trusting and empowering teams
- knowledgeable business stakeholders are available to work with the project team throughout the project lifecycle
- the technology platform that the team is using supports incremental delivery
- there are no restrictions in current contractual arrangements that make it difficult (if not impossible) to support Agile methods.

If your project does not fully meet these criteria, you may still be positioned to get some benefit from using Agile methods. For example, if the technology platform that the team is using does not support incremental delivery of functionality (e.g. fixed enterprise platforms, legacy systems, bundled systems, restrictive third-party products), the team can focus their work

---

[31] Organizations with highly predictable and replicable processes may achieve greater benefit from the use of *lean manufacturing* techniques to minimize their overheads in these processes. See More Information on Agile for resources on lean manufacturing.

on the highest priority capabilities using time-boxed intervals, but the benefits of *leveraging what they are building in a live environment* may be restricted to the end of the project (or may not occur at all if the project is ended earlier than expected).

Dispelling Agile myths

Agile is a 'quick fix' solution

Implementing Agile methods in your organization will not change your IT balance sheet from red to black in a matter of weeks, or even months. Time is needed for staff to become familiar with these approaches; to refine their use of Agile to align with the specific requirements of your organization; and to organically grow the use of Agile to a sufficiently critical mass of IT projects that can offset the losses from traditionally managed software projects.

Instead, think of Agile as an *investment* in your organization's IT future, particularly in reducing the whole-of-life costs of maintaining, supporting and extending the software solutions that you deliver.

Agile projects do not require planning

Agile methods have, at times, received an unjustified reputation for being an 'ad hoc' approach to software delivery. However, nothing could be further from the truth. In reality, Agile methods replace one-time up-front planning with the *ongoing* refinement, re-confirmation and adjustment of plans throughout the delivery process to reflect the most current information available to the organization. In this way, Agile surpasses more traditional approaches that rely upon a large up-front plan which is likely to become obsolete by the time it reaches the printer.

Agile projects do not require documentation

In the same way that Agile methods have been mistakenly believed to be 'ad hoc' software development approaches without proper planning, these methods also fall victim to the misunderstanding that they can be implemented without system or business documentation. This is also untrue. Agile practitioners understand that organizations rely on formal documentation for compliance purposes, as a record of communication, etc. In fact, for some Agile methods, such as DSDM, the production of formal documentation (e.g. the Feasibility Report) is a mandatory requirement for teams to progress to the next stage of work.

The difference with Agile methods is that *active face-to-face* communication is generally the preferred method for exchanging information; whereas formal documentation is produced to the extent that it is appropriate for the organization.

For example, Agile teams prefer to replace the need for extensive formal system requirements documentation with *interactive sessions* where participants can discuss business and technical requirements face to face, ask targeted questions, and provide direct feedback to refine these requirements. The 'documentation' of these sessions is generally done through the ongoing production of *working software* that reflects the outcome of the discussions.

Where formal requirements documentation is required by the organization, it is often produced retrospectively, during (or even after) the release of the system. This not only allows the team to focus on their core work during the development process, it results in documentation which is often more cost-effective to produce (e.g. by using screen captures from the actual system), and which tends to better reflect the actual behavior of the released system.

Agile projects are unmanaged

Agile methods encourage a different form of management than traditional organizations may be used to. Instead of top-down mandates and closely monitored staff, project teams are empowered to do the work that is required under the guidance and oversight of stakeholders. This results in the establishment of *self-organized* teams.

The following quote from General George S. Patton, Jr. is an amazing testament to the power of self-organized teams:

Never tell people how to do things. Tell them what to do and they will surprise you with their ingenuity.

Even in a military environment, General Patton understood the value of directing his troops and then trusting them to get the job done. Agile methods are based upon the same underlying premise of both guiding and empowering people in order to get the most value from their work.

Self-organized teams can provide the organization with several benefits, including:

- planning based on specialist, hands-on knowledge of the work that is required to achieve business objectives
- more realistic estimates of the work that the team can achieve
- motivation for the team to want to achieve the work that they have actively committed to
- natural skills and strengths compensation, where teams divide and conquer the work required based on the relative skills and strengths of each team member.

Management is able to oversee the productivity and value of each project team's work through Agile measuring and monitoring tools, such as executive dashboards, product backlogs and Kanban boards. Arguably, however, the most definitive method of measuring results is the team's ongoing production of tangible, high business-value outcomes.

Agile is too risky (or radical) for our organization

The idea of implementing approaches that:

- encourage the evolution of business requirements, instead of relying upon up-front signed-off documentation
- empower the team to self-organize, instead of controlling their daily activities
- replace reams of documentation with face-to-face communication

may seem a bit daunting for some executives (and terms like *eXtreme Programming* probably do not do much to allay these concerns).

The *Who uses Agile?* section in the previous chapter identified a number of highly reputable organizations worldwide that use Agile methods, including several (e.g. Microsoft™, Yahoo!™) that have published case studies documenting the benefits of these approaches. These are not rogue start-up organizations with radical notions of success; they are organizations with structured key performance indicators (KPIs), bottom-line imperatives and accountability to shareholders. If Agile methods are able to deliver significant business-value benefits to these organizations, it is reasonable to expect comparable returns in your organization. The challenge is in turning these benefits into *ROI metrics* that align with the specific challenges that your organization is facing.

Your Agile ROI

Identifying the potential return on your Agile investment ('your Agile ROI') is contingent upon four primary factors:

- the *business value* that your software solutions generate
- your current costs to *develop* and *implement* software solutions
- your current costs to *support*, *maintain* and *extend* the software solutions that you deliver
- your current costs in *managing staff turnover*, including hiring costs, re-skilling, and loss of corporate memory.

Although there are indirect costs involved in calculating *your Agile ROI*, such as the loss of *prospective* business due to problems in previously delivered software solutions, the four primary factors above represent the most tangible (and quantifiable) costs for you to consider in your decision to implement (or not to implement) Agile methods.

The ROI that your organization can expect to achieve by implementing Agile methods is directly aligned to the *10 core*

Agile business benefits identified in the previous chapter, specifically:

For ***both*** *commercial and in-house software solutions:*

- Containment of software development and implementation costs by:
    - reducing the risk of development budgets being squandered on low business-value or misaligned features
    - reducing the risk of software development budget blow-outs due to technical and architectural issues that are discovered only after significant investment has been made
    - controlling ongoing budget expenditure at each iteration by deciding to proceed with, adjust, postpone, or stop ongoing iterations based on the business value of demonstrated results to date.
- Greater ongoing return on software development investments by:
    - receiving valuable, tangible outcomes every month, instead of waiting until the end of a year-long initiative before any ROI is achieved
    - accommodating organizational, industry and technology changes throughout the software development process, so that previously undertaken work can retain much of its business value.
- Reduction in whole-of-life software costs by:
    - minimizing the potential for software errors, usability issues, or misalignment with business needs
    - increasing the extensibility of the software solution to accommodate ongoing changes.
- Reduction in employee turnover rates (project team members) by giving them a more positive, rewarding and supportive work environment, with fewer last-minute 'fire-fighting' activities that create unnecessary stress in the workplace.

In addition, organizations who deliver *commercial software solutions* can expect to achieve the following ROI benefits:

- greater customer retention rates (and potential for add-on sales) by consistently delivering higher-quality software solutions that are more relevant to customer needs
- stronger market positioning for the positive reputation that results from the delivery of higher quality and more relevant software solutions.

Similarly, organizations who deliver *in-house software solutions* can expect to achieve the following additional ROI benefits:

- reduction in operational costs by having software solutions that more closely align with the needs of the business
- a corresponding reduction in the employee turnover rates of *business users* by providing a work environment that encourages the communication of their requirements, and software solutions that genuinely meet their ongoing needs.

It is important to note that the introduction of Agile methods is *not* likely to result in a substantial decrease in *software development* costs. In fact, in the initial implementation of these approaches, there are likely to be *additional* overheads associated with training and knowledge sharing, establishing supporting technologies (e.g. automated testing environments), and establishing centralized locations for teams to work and collaborate.

Instead, Agile methods are far more likely to result in cost savings by delivering software solutions that are of a significantly higher quality, have far greater usability, and are much more aligned to the highest priority business needs of the organization.

Therefore, the most relevant ROI calculation for your organization is not likely to be a side-by-side comparison of *software development* costs for projects using traditional processes versus Agile methods; it is a side-by-side comparison of the *whole-of-life* costs of *developing, maintaining, supporting* and *extending* each of these software solutions, as well as tracking turnover rates for both IT staff and (where appropriate) the business areas utilizing these solutions.

In Chapter 3: Five Steps to Agile Success, strategies and guidelines are provided to enable you to measure quantitative and qualitative returns from your organization's Agile work.

Your organizational culture

Earlier in this chapter, it was identified that Agile methods are not for every organization, explaining that dynamic organizations and organizations with unsustainable IT overheads are better positioned to receive more substantial benefits from using these approaches. There is, however, another element in the 'Is Agile right for my organization?' equation: your organizational culture.

In order to determine if Agile methods are truly suited to your organization, you need to ask yourself the following three critical questions:

- Is management willing to trust staff to get work done without constant supervision?
- Could the structure and culture of the organization support a distributed, self-organizing team management model, i.e. where management is *not* at the center of all activity?
- Is the organization prepared to change their 'business as usual' routines?

If the answer to any of these questions is *No*, then implementing Agile methods in your organization may be a challenge (if not an impossibility) without a significant change in your organizational culture. Thankfully, you are likely to be in a far better position than others in your organization to institute this change.

The following sections outline the core cultural factors that are necessary for Agile methods to succeed in your organization.

Trusting the team

At the heart of Agile methods is the firm belief that people can – and will – do the right thing by the organization if they are given the opportunity. If the senior management of an organization sees employees as unmotivated people who have to be supervised closely in order to get any work done, they will be far less willing to entrust teams to self-organize. (The irony is that these same managers rarely appreciate that a corporate culture of mistrust breeds unmotivated people.)

Agile methods rely on the mutual trust (and dependency) that emerges between stakeholders and project team members:

- project teams depend upon the expertise of stakeholders to accurately identify, communicate and prioritize the business requirements
- stakeholders equally depend upon the expertise of the project team members to regularly produce outcomes that meet these requirements.

The stakeholders determine what high-priority goals the organization needs to meet; the project team determines what high-priority work they are in a position to deliver, and the technical solution which is best suited to achieve these goals. If either group falters, the process fails.

Equally important is the establishment of trust *within* the project teams. Open communication, skills and strengths compensation, and camaraderie can only be achieved in a work environment that values teamwork and discourages finger pointing. If the team is not working as a cohesive whole, then the benefits of Agile methods may be lost before the process even begins.

Relinquishing the need for management to control everything

In Dispelling Agile Myths, it was identified that self-organized teams are ideally positioned to provide the organization with:

- specialist, hands-on knowledge of the actual work required (versus top-down mandates from managers with more limited knowledge of the technology)
- more realistic estimates of the work that can be achieved (versus 'paper plans' that are based on assumed levels of productivity, and a limited awareness of staff throughput levels or competing staff commitments)

- motivation for the team to want to achieve the work that they have actively committed to (versus the work that is thrust upon them)
- natural skills and strengths compensation (versus allocating roles, responsibilities and recognition to individual members of the team).

It was further identified that the structure of Agile methods means that managers do not need to keep a close watch on every step that the team makes, because they know that they are never more than a few weeks away from seeing the tangible results of their work.

The interesting thing about the dynamic of self-organizing teams is that, as they progress, they are able to create *ongoing* motivation for employees. Project team members know that their continued ability to self-manage their work depends on their regular delivery of high-value business outcomes. Additionally, because they are the ones who identify what work can (and cannot) be achieved in each iteration, they are motivated by their personal responsibility to achieve these outcomes. This combination of factors is heightened by the satisfaction and pride that team members feel when they produce tangible outputs that truly meet the needs of the organization.

Therefore, in order for Agile methods to work, managers who have traditionally maintained heavy-handed control over the day-to-day work of their staff will need to be willing to relinquish that control in favor of trusting and empowering their staff. As an executive, the power rests in your hands to promote this shift in management style, or to strategically select the right managers when introducing Agile projects to the organization. (See *Choosing the right kick-off point* for further information on selecting the most suitable Agile projects for your organization.)

Eliminating the 'business as usual' mindset

There is no doubt that Agile methods require organizations to act – and think – differently to the way that they have in the past. Those organizations that are self-aware (and humble) enough to recognize that their business practices of the past may not sustain them into the future, will be more amenable to considering Agile methods, especially given their widespread support and long history of success. In contrast, employers who are committed to 'the way we do things around here' are likely to see Agile approaches as too radical for their organization. The bottom line is that Agile methods are a significant change in the way in which an organization will operate – but change can be for the *better*.

Even if your organization is facing all three of these cultural barriers, it is important to realize that they are not insurmountable obstacles. There are proven approaches for laying the groundwork that will allow your organizational culture to support Agile methods. In *Chapter 3: Five Steps to Agile Success*, guidelines are provided for selecting, implementing and expanding Agile projects to suit even the most conservative organizations.

Your decision

The decision to shift to (or even trial) a new way of doing business can be daunting for any organization. There may be inefficiencies in your current business processes – and times when you wish that staff were more productive – but is this enough of an argument to forego the 'devil you know' in favor of unchartered territory? Moreover, even if you are convinced that your organization has room for improvement, that does not necessarily mean that moving to Agile methods is the answer.

Agile methods may seem like a radical shift for some organizations, but they have also been proven to produce radically improved outcomes for those organizations that have applied them.

The most compelling argument in favor of trialling Agile methods is the fact that it costs your organization very little to get started. In the same way that Agile protects the organization from the risk of large up-front commitments, it equally does not require a large up-front commitment from the organization in order to be used. This can make trialling Agile approaches in an organization a cost-contained activity, which the organization can opt to expand (or reduce) without having jeopardized a significant financial investment.

In *Chapter 3: Five Steps to Agile Success*, strategies and guidelines are provided to help your organization choose the right starting point for introducing Agile methods, for baselining and monitoring the ROI in your Agile projects, and for expanding the use of Agile, as appropriate, to meet the ongoing needs of your organization.

CHAPTER 3: FIVE STEPS TO AGILE SUCCESS

Step One: Choosing the right kick-off point

Although it might be tempting for you to want to 'dive right in' and start using an Agile method (e.g. Scrum) to salvage your struggling software projects, it is valuable for you to step back for a moment and consider the specific needs – and constraints – of your organization.

Choosing the right project(s)

Deciding *where to begin* using Agile methods in your organization is as important as deciding which method you will use. In addition to the criteria for project success identified in the *Agile is not for every project* section, you need to consider the following questions:

Is your objective to do a 'safe' trial of Agile before committing to its broader use across the organization? If so, you may want to select a self-contained new software development project which will not be unduly burdened by the constraints of legacy systems or pre-existing project management techniques. Provide the team with a clean slate to start from, and then use the ROI metrics described in the *Monitoring your investment* section of this chapter to measure the results.

Is your objective to create some 'runs on the board' to influence others in the organization to consider using Agile methods? If so, then you need to choose projects that are important enough so that their success will be meaningful to the organization. Achieving great results on trivial projects will only serve to fuel resistance from others in the organization who may believe that Agile methods are not applicable to their IT projects.

Is your objective to mandate the immediate use of Agile methods for all software development work across the organization? If so, you will need to review the information about organizations who have successfully achieved this in the *Choosing the right method of introduction* section.

Is your objective to use Agile methods to begin to shift the organizational culture towards a more open and collaborative environment? If so, you may want to start with the path of least cultural resistance by choosing an area of the organization which (or a particular manager who) is most likely to be amenable to working closely with stakeholders, trusting and empowering teams, and measuring success through the production and demonstration of tangible results.

Once you have selected the project(s) that align with your core objectives, the next step is determining which Agile methods and practices are best suited to the needs of the selected project(s).

Choosing the right methods and practices

Agile methods are not a 'one size fits all' proposition. For these approaches to deliver genuine business value to your organization, it is important to find the right Agile method (or combination of methods and practices) to address your specific challenges, your KPIs and your culture. It is equally important to work with the selected project teams in making this decision.

The Agile methods selection workflow tool in Figure 2 takes you through some of the key questions that you need to ask in order to select the most appropriate Agile methods and practices for each of your selected projects.[32]

It is important to note that the Agile methods selection workflow tool is only a guideline for you to use as a starting point in selecting the methods and practices that are more likely to be suited to the unique requirements of your project and your organization. Your ongoing use of these approaches is the definitive indicator of how well they meet your needs.

---

[32] The Agile methods selection workflow tool only addresses the ten Agile methods described in the *Common Agile methods* section of Chapter 1. It does not include Disciplined Agile Delivery, Crystal or other methods which may be equally valuable to your organization.

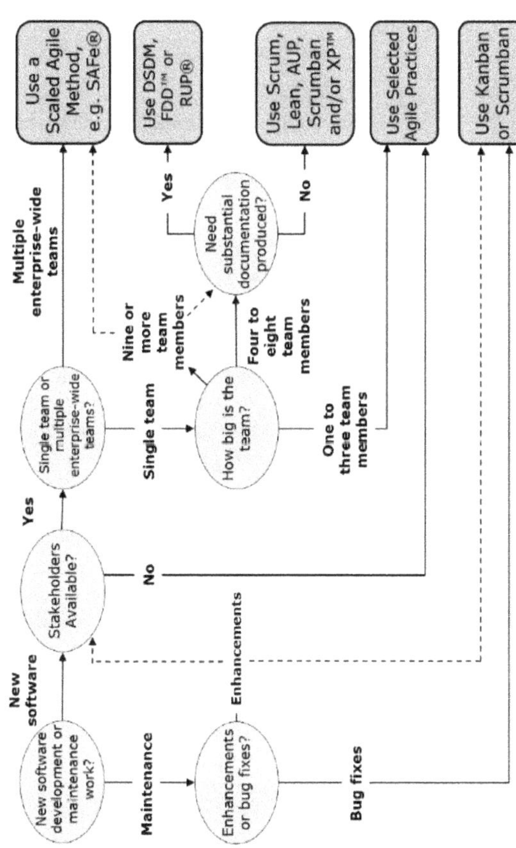

Figure 2: The Agile methods selection workflow tool

To use the Agile methods selection workflow tool, start with the question in the upper left-hand corner:

New Software Development or Maintenance Work?

If the project that you have selected is a new software development, then go to the **Stakeholders Available?** question below.

If the project is predominantly a maintenance activity, then the next question to consider is whether or not the maintenance work will include the development of **Enhancements or Bug Fixes?**

If the project is a maintenance activity primarily for bug fixes, you may be best off starting with ***Kanban*** or ***Scrumban*** to manage this work.

If the project is a maintenance activity that includes a significant number of enhancements, you may decide, instead, to treat these enhancements as new software development; in which case, you will want to go to the **Stakeholders Available?** question in the following section.

Stakeholders Available?

Almost every aspect of Agile methods requires involvement from the stakeholders (e.g. business areas, customers) who will be using the delivered software. If these stakeholders are unavailable (and your organization is not in a position to make them available, or to organize for other resources who can adequately represent their interests), then your options for using Agile methods are extremely limited. Therefore, if the answer to the **Stakeholders Available?** question is *No*, the project team may be able to utilize some selected Agile practices, such as daily stand-up meetings, time-boxed work, pair programming or test-driven development, to enhance the quality and throughput of their development work; but the substantial benefits of using Agile methods to deliver usable software solutions that directly align to customer needs will not be achieved.

Single team or multiple enterprise-wide teams?

If you intend to implement your selected Agile method within a single development team, then go to the **How big is the team?** question below.

If you intend to implement Agile methods across multiple enterprise-wide teams, you may want to consider using one of the scaled Agile methods, such as ***SAFe®***, ***Scrum of Scrums***, the ***Large Scale Scrum (LeSS) framework*** or ***Nexus***. Ideally, you will have successfully implemented Agile methods on a smaller scale *before* endeavoring to implement a large scale Agile initiative. This allows you to leverage the lessons learned, the skills acquired and the cultural adaptations made at a smaller scale, which will increase the likelihood of successfully integrating Agile work across multiple teams - and decrease the potential for unaddressed issues to grow exponentially.

How big is the team?

It is generally believed that the ideal size for a single team using Agile methods, such as Scrum, is four to eight team members (although this is not a hard-and-fast rule). If your intended team has four to eight members, then go to the **Need substantial documentation produced?** question below.

If you have fewer than four members on your team for the selected project, it may be better for your organization to consider using selected Agile practices (noting that at least two coders will be required for pair programming).

If you have more than eight team members, you may want to consider breaking down the teams into groups of four to eight, and then scaling the project work for the selected Agile method(s). Alternatively, you can opt to progress as a single, larger team and select the most appropriate Agile method by progressing to the **Need substantial documentation produced?** question below.

Need substantial documentation produced?

The final question to ask yourself is whether or not the organization (or you personally) prefer for the work undertaken by project teams to be substantially documented throughout the process. If so, it may be better for you to use Agile methods such as ***DSDM***, ***FDD***™ or ***RUP***® which mandate the generation of work products, such as requirements specifications and domain models, as part of the process. Otherwise, it may be better for you to start with methods such as ***Scrum***, ***Lean***, ***AUP***, ***Scrumban*** or ***XP***™ (or combinations of these), as they are more flexible to accommodate each team's preferred work practices and levels of documentation.

If you have selected more than one project as your starting point, it may be valuable for you to trial two or three different Agile methods at the same time to see which is the best fit for your organization.

Last, in selecting Agile methods for your organization to trial, you need to be prepared to allow staff to *adjust* and *modify* their use of these methods to achieve their optimal levels of productivity as their work progresses. For example, project teams may not, at first, be comfortable with committing to the two- to four-week delivery cycle of Scrum; in which case, the team may be better off using a six- to eight-week cycle as a starting point. Equally, team members may not have enough information at hand to do the value stream mapping that Lean requires, but they may be able to identify and address immediate areas of waste in the current software development processes. The key is to give teams the power to adapt the *practices* of Agile without jeopardizing the underlying *principles*. (See the Avoiding common traps section for further detail on the perils of the *misapplication* of Agile methods.)

Choosing the right method of introduction

In a perfect world, the introduction of Agile methods within your organization would be achieved through an organization-wide mandate where staff readily embraced and adopted these approaches. In reality, however, the opportunity to achieve organization-wide Agile adoption as a starting point may be rare, but it is not impossible.

BT Innovate & Design provides a classic example of an organization who successfully achieved organization-wide Agile adoption courtesy of a forward-thinking executive who, in 2004, established a mandate that the organization produce business value every 90 days.[33]

It should be noted that the BT example is an exceptional situation. It is far more common for Agile methods and practices to be introduced to an organization by the team members themselves, often without the active awareness (or support) of senior management. (You may, in fact, be surprised to learn that there are IT project teams within your organization who are already using Agile.) This 'Agile by Stealth' approach is generally not the team's preferred way of introducing Agile within the organization; they would much rather have your support and backing for this work. Instead, this approach is likely to be perceived by the team members as a necessary way to ensure that they can progress with these practices 'under the radar' without provoking management resistance or challenging the traditional approaches of the organization.

If, in your discussions with prospective Agile teams, you find that they have already been utilizing these methods, you are likely to be one step ahead of the game. In most cases, these teams will not have definitive ROI metrics for the work that they have done to date (see *Establishing your baseline* and *Monitoring your investment* for further detail on measuring ROI). They are, however, likely to have a number of work products, including Agile communication tools, delivered software, and stakeholder testimonials, which can indicate how well their selected Agile methods worked. They are also likely to have acquired a substantial amount of knowledge about what does – and does not – work within your organizational culture.

---

[33] Details on the approach that BT successfully used is provided in the *Avoiding common traps* section of this chapter, with further details available at *Agile Coaching in British Telecom*, Meadows L and Hanly S (2006): *www.agileconnection.com/article/agile-coaching-british-telecom*

All of this information can be applied to selecting the best ongoing approaches for your organization to use, including the expansion of the team's Agile work with the benefit of your support.

If your organization is not planning to issue organization-wide mandates to adopt Agile, and you have not been fortunate enough to unearth Agile success stories within your organization, the next best thing is the selection of one or more trial projects, using the guidelines in Choosing the right project(s) section. Tracking and documenting the outcomes of these trial projects can be used as the basis for persuading other areas of the organization to consider Agile methods for their projects. (See the Expanding Agile section for further details.)

You may also choose to position yourself as an Agile champion within the organization, using industry case studies (such as Microsoft™ and Yahoo!™) and industry research (such as VersionOne™) to support your decision to trial these approaches. Your awareness of Agile methods, coupled with your influence, can help to position Agile teams to avoid the most common traps that organizations encounter in their implementation of Agile methods, as described in the following.

Step Two: Avoiding common traps

The simplicity and low overheads that make using Agile methods so appealing, also make them highly susceptible to misapplication. The following identifies some of the most common traps that organizations have fallen into when implementing Agile.

Undermining Agile principles

There is a difference between adapting Agile to suit the preferred work practices of your organization (e.g. adjusting iteration timeframes, using videoconferencing instead of face-to-face meetings), and adapting Agile in a way that contravenes the underlying principles that drive its effectiveness.

One example is an organization that moves to an 'Agile' iteration-based project management model, but still requires all of the work to be signed-off in an up-front specification. Agile methods are only valuable when the organization is in a position to *adapt* ongoing work as it progresses. Otherwise, iterative work just becomes shorter delivery cycles that are limited by the same core constraints; and Agile methods get an unjustified bad reputation when this pre-constrained process inevitably fails.

Similarly dangerous is an organization that applies a handful of Agile practices (e.g. daily stand-up meetings, test-driven development) without the benefit of the core elements of each Agile method, such as stakeholder confirmation of requirements, or the ongoing adjustment of work to accommodate emerging information. In the Agile methods selection workflow tool, it was identified that, for projects without stakeholder availability, the use of selected Agile practices may be the only option available to the team. By using selected Agile practices, however, the outcome is likely to be a somewhat more efficient traditional software development process, not an Agile project.

Insufficient communication and/or training

In order for Agile to be effective, participants (stakeholders and project team members) need to be educated on the principles and practices of the selected method. Otherwise, they (and the organization) are likely to fall victim to the areas of misapplication identified in the previous section.

In Choosing the right method of introduction, the Agile work undertaken at BT Innovate & Design was referenced as a classic example of the successful organization-wide adoption of Agile based on a top-down executive mandate. What was not mentioned, however, was *how* this success was achieved.

When the CIO of the organization established the mandate for the use of Agile throughout the organization, he coupled that mandate with a series of training and communication initiatives to educate staff on Agile principles and practices. These initiatives included training and learning events (e.g. roadshows), assigning Agile coaches, and creating *The BT Agile Cookbook* as an online reference guide for staff. BT's continued use of these practices in the organization several years later is a testament to the power of both initial and ongoing communication – as well as the importance of genuine management commitment – in the successful implementation of Agile.

When introducing Agile in your organization, it is important to consider how Agile principles and practices will be communicated to staff. One cost-effective way to achieve this is by including an Agile resources page on your corporate intranet that provides links to relevant sites, and allows staff to exchange their questions, concerns and ideas about the use of these methods before work begins.

Alternatively, your organization may benefit from more formal guidance on adopting and applying Agile methods. There are a number of formal training courses available to teach people how to more effectively apply Agile methods. In some cases (e.g. Scrum) there are even certification courses that staff can attend.

All of these communication approaches help to assure you that your selected Agile methods are being utilized to the greatest advantage of the organization.

Using Agile as a doctrine instead of a tool

This last common area of misapplication was alluded to in *Choosing the right kick-off point*: following Agile as a strict doctrine without adapting it to the needs of your organization. To receive the greatest benefit from using Agile methods, it is important to allow your staff to adjust and modify their use of these methods in a way that fits in with their preferred work practices. That is, so long as the underlying principles of Agile are not compromised.

As you are introducing (and trialling) Agile methods within your organization, it is valuable to consider the advice provided by the author of *Kanban and Scrum: making the most of both*[34] who noted that:

Scrum [Agile] is just a tool. You choose when and how to use it. Don't be a slave to it!

However you and your staff choose to introduce Agile within your organization, you can (and should) adapt it to suit your specific needs. By its very nature, Agile methods are meant to be, well, *agile*.

Step Three: Establishing your baseline

Throughout the previous chapters, the term *ROI metrics* has been used as a mechanism for quantifying the business value that Agile methods can deliver to your organization. The following gives you a step-by-step approach for identifying the quantitative and qualitative value of your current work as a baseline for measuring the impact of implementing Agile methods for your future projects.

Calculating the net business value of current project work

In order to measure the comparative ROI value from the implementation of Agile, your organization needs to be able to assess and record the *net business value* of equivalent work activities prior to its introduction. For example, a software project, which was delivered using your current software development processes, and which is similar in scope and complexity to the software that is being proposed for your intended Agile project (i.e. your 'comparison project'). The business value of your *comparison project* can then represent the baseline for future ROI comparison.

Identifying the potential *quantitative net business value* return on your Agile investment is, from my experience, contingent upon four primary factors:

- the *business value* that your software solutions generate

[34] *Kanban and Scrum: making the most of both*, Kniberg, Henrik (2010): www.infoq.com/minibooks/kanban-scrum-minibook

- your current costs to *develop* and *implement* software solutions
- your current costs to *support, maintain* and *extend* the software solutions that you deliver
- your current costs in *managing staff turnover.*

In order to baseline the quantitative net business value of your *comparison project*, you will need to gather the following metrics:

- a quantifiable business value for that project's delivered software features, based on revenue generated and/or reductions in operational overheads (***software value***)
- the overhead costs for software development and implementation on that project, e.g. staff, accommodation, equipment (***delivery overhead***)
- the *non-recoverable*[35] overhead costs for software support, maintenance and extension of that project (***non-recoverable support overhead***)
- the average cost for replacing an IT staff member who has left the organization (***IT staff turnover cost***)
- the percentage of IT staff turnover that can be reasonably aligned to the resources allocated to that project (***IT staff turnover percentage***).

[35] As many IT projects pre-allocate funding for warranty period work and/or charge back annual support costs, non-recoverable costs refer to the portion of software maintenance work that cannot be recovered from allocated funds. There is, however, an argument to say that pre-allocated funding for software support should be focused on upgraded features and enhancements; in which case, the cost of bug fixes within these funds should also be considered non-recoverable.

Then apply these metrics, using the following **software project net business value** formula:

$$\text{Software Value} - \text{Delivery Overhead} - \text{Non-Recoverable Support Overhead} - \left(\text{IT Staff Turnover Cost} \times \text{\% of IT Staff Turnover}\right) = \text{Software Project Net Business Value}$$

Figure 3: Software project net business value formula

The resulting figure represents the ***quantitative net business value*** for your *comparison project.*

To provide you with the most complete assessment of business value, these quantitative metrics should be coupled with qualitative metrics on:

- how satisfied your stakeholders (external customers, internal business areas) are with delivered software
- how satisfied your IT staff members are with their current work environment
- how often teams are working overtime or 'fire-fighting' to address software problems.

Compensating for insufficient metrics

The purest ROI comparison scenario would involve the establishment of two identical projects, each using the same objectives, the same budget allocation and the same number of employees, in the same timeframe: where one would be undertaken using your organization's current software development processes; the other, using your selected Agile method. In order to minimize the impact of external factors, this scenario would also involve the isolation of staff from all other commitments during this time. In my 25 years of working in the industry, however, I have never encountered a situation that supported this scenario.

More realistically, organizations tend to find themselves with a combination of the following baseline information sources for their current projects:

- high-level budget reports (e.g. department or project expenditure breakdowns)
- incremental project status reports (with minimal quantitative metrics)
- sales figures and customer surveys (for commercial organizations with released software)
- issue registers and, where software is in production use, support logs
- anecdotal evidence of the success or failure of software development projects.

Therefore, in order to baseline the ***quantitative net business value*** for your *comparison project* (i.e. business value; costs for development, implementation, non-recoverable support and maintenance; and staff turnover), you need to determine whether the metrics that your organization currently record are sufficient.

If you can confidently assess (or reasonably estimate) your *comparison project* costs, then you should be well positioned to calculate your Agile ROI on an equivalent project undertaken using Agile methods.

If you are not confident that your *comparison project* costs can be sufficiently assessed, then you need to decide if:

- you are comfortable proceeding with partial baseline information
- you would like to track the business value of your proposed Agile implementation without a baseline comparison
- you would prefer to gather baseline metrics on a current (or planned) software project *before* proceeding with the Agile implementation.

If you do decide to proceed with the information at hand, it may be valuable to establish a framework for tracking the ***quantitative net business value*** of Agile projects on an ongoing basis, so that you can measure the relative effectiveness of selected methods, as well as any changes in the levels of productivity and business value produced as staff become more familiar with these approaches.

Step Four: Monitoring your investment

Once you have established the baseline metrics for your current work (or have identified an alternative approach where your current metrics are insufficient), you are in a position to begin assessing the comparative value of your Agile work.

Tracking the progress of your Agile projects

Monitoring the business value and progress of your Agile projects can begin from the moment the project starts, and continue well before the whole-of-life ***quantitative net business value*** is evident.

Agile methods provide a number of mechanisms for tracking progress, including formal reports (e.g. executive dashboards), status update tools (e.g. WIP boards, product backlogs, sprint backlogs), and ongoing communication with stakeholders. Arguably, however, the most valuable measure of the Agile team's progress is their delivery of *tangible outputs*. For iterative Agile methods, such as Scrum and FDD™, the presentation of working software occurs at the end of each iteration. This means that, at fixed timeframes (generally once a month), you are able to see firsthand whether these approaches are delivering their anticipated business value.

Equally important, the teams themselves are able to use Agile tools to monitor their own progress during each iteration, and to adjust their ongoing work as needed to meet their agreed commitments.

It is interesting to note that the timing of four-week iterations aligns closely with the timing of monthly reports. This means that Agile teams may be able to use the presentation of working software at the end of each four-week iteration to report on their progress in conjunction with the standard reporting cycles for the organization overall (where required).

Comparing Agile to your current software development processes

If you have baselined the ***quantitative net business value*** for your *comparison project* (see Establishing your baseline), then comparing that project with the ***quantitative net business value*** of an *equivalent Agile project* is a straightforward ROI calculation – well, almost.

Retrospective comparison between two software solutions that are both in a production environment is reasonably achievable, as long as the variables (e.g. length of time in production) can be normalized.

The challenge (or opportunity) arises when comparing traditional software development projects that are *in progress* with equivalent Agile projects. The whole-of-life costs for software (including ongoing maintenance, support and extension costs) are not able to be measured until after the software has been *released.* For traditional software development projects, this is generally only available *at the end of the process*, i.e. when the complete software solution is implemented in a live production environment. For Agile projects, particularly ones using iterative approaches, software features can be released for production use on an *ongoing* basis. This means that you are in a position to track ***quantitative net business value*** of your *equivalent Agile project* well before that information is available for your *comparison project*. For this reason, it is recommended that your selected *comparison project* be a historical project (i.e. one that is already in production).

A cautionary note: As explained in the Your Agile ROI section of Chapter 2, the most relevant ROI calculation for your organization is not likely to be a side-by-side comparison of *software development* costs for projects using traditional processes versus Agile methods; it is a side-by-side comparison of the *whole-of-life* costs of *developing, maintaining, supporting* and *extending* each of these software solutions.

Thus far, the focus of the comparison between traditional and Agile software development projects has been focused on the relative *quantitative* benefits between these approaches. It is just as (if not more) important to compare the *qualitative* benefits as well, including:

- the impact that each approach has had on employee motivation, camaraderie and job satisfaction, particularly for the project team members
- stakeholder response to the usability and relevance of the delivered software
- the impact that each approach has had on management.

Many of the benefits of Agile go well beyond what can be tracked on a balance sheet.

Comparing business value across Agile methods

If you have established a framework for tracking the ***quantitative net business value*** of Agile projects, then comparing your ROI across different Agile methods is also a relatively straightforward calculation. The important distinction is that you need to find a reasonable 'apples-to-apples' comparison between equivalent Agile methods. For example, Scrum and DSDM are both centered around iterative project delivery based on stakeholder feedback, so it is reasonable to compare outputs from these two methods side-by-side. Conversely, XP and Kanban are Agile methods with different functions (and outputs) to iterative project delivery. Therefore, it is more difficult to establish a meaningful ROI comparison between these Agile methods and iterative project delivery methodologies.

In comparing different Agile methods, it is especially important to compare the *qualitative* benefits as well, particularly to identify project team and stakeholder reactions to each method. Were staff happier with the formal documentation structure of DSDM, or did they find that Scrum tools and practices were sufficient to communicate requirements? Were they comfortable using the pair programming practices of XP? What were the biggest challenges in each method? Are there any areas where they would like more formal training or expert advice (e.g. how to manage a product backlog)? Staff input is critical to undertaking the Agile evolution tracking activities described in the following section.

Tracking Agile evolution

As identified in <u>*Your Agile ROI*</u>, when you first introduce Agile methods in your organization, there are likely to be *additional* overheads associated with training and knowledge sharing; establishing supporting technologies (e.g. automated testing environments); and establishing centralized locations for project teams to work and collaborate. As Agile work progresses, staff members will become more comfortable with (and proficient in) these practices, and the methods that they use will most likely be adapted to work more effectively in your organizational climate. All of these factors contribute to the ability of Agile methods to provide the organization with even greater business value as they evolve.

The framework that you have devised for tracking the ***quantitative net business value*** of Agile projects becomes a toolset that you can use to track the relative net business value of initial Agile projects against projects run by established Agile teams. This not only enables you to see progress in your Agile work, it provides you with a mechanism for undertaking *predictive analysis* if you decide to extend the use of Agile in your organization. (See <u>*Expanding Agile*</u> for further details.)

In addition, the qualitative metrics that you have been gathering for each Agile method (e.g. what challenges the teams faced and how they overcame them) can be transformed into guidelines, lessons learned and customized training materials for staff to use in other Agile projects.

Don't be fooled by the numbers

Although this section focused primarily on identifying baseline ROI metrics for *quantitative* comparison, monitoring your Agile investment is much more than a numbers game. Comparative whole-of-life software development costs will give you an indication of the bottom-line business value of

Agile, but they will not help you to find the root cause of software errors, usability issues and misalignment with business requirements; nor will they help you to understand the team's dynamics or frustrations. These indicators tend to emerge in more insidious ways, as emergency software patches, lost customers, or valued members of your IT staff deciding to leave the organization. Successfully addressing these issues is the *immeasurable* benefit of Agile methods.

Step Five: Expanding Agile

After your organization has had the opportunity to trial Agile methods for a few months, it is valuable for you to step back and ask yourself the following questions:

- Is work being done more efficiently?
- Are the stakeholders getting the outcomes that they need?
- Are employees happier to be working in a high-communication environment, rather than in a documentation-centric one?
- Is the quality of their work better than before?

The answers to these questions – in addition to the ROI comparisons described in the previous section – should provide you with sufficient information to consider broadening the use of Agile methods to other areas of the organization. (Or, conversely, to decide that Agile methods are not suited to your organization and should not be extended further; in which case, the low start-up costs of Agile have enabled you to make that decision without foregoing a huge up-front investment.)

If you decide to expand the use of Agile methods to other areas of the organization, the next step is to establish a strategy for broadening awareness of the value of Agile methods across the organization – and for encouraging other areas to trial these approaches.[36]

This strategy should include four key elements:

[36] That is, unless you decide to issue an organization-wide Agile mandate, as BT did.

- ***Education:*** communicating with the organization on the quantitative and qualitative *business value* of Agile methods (using your ROI metrics, team feedback, etc.). This can be done through:
  - internal 'roadshow' events to show people the tangible outcomes from your Agile work
  - your corporate intranet (as described in <u>*Avoiding common traps*</u>)
  - documenting the outcomes of your trial project as a case study for other groups in the organization.
- ***Motivation:*** using the information above, along with your influence, to encourage specific people in the organization to trial these methods in their areas (e.g. those who are more open to trying new approaches, or those who have had historical problems with their software development projects).
- ***Selection:*** helping interested areas of the organization in selecting the Agile method(s) that are best suited to their activities (using the <u>*Agile methods selection workflow*</u> tool). The metrics gathered in the previous section can also help these areas to undertake *predictive analysis* on initial and ongoing costs and ROI benefits for each method.
- ***Collaboration:*** providing assistance (and, where appropriate, experienced Agile team members) to help each area in the initial application of these methods. This includes educating the area on the principles and practices of their selected Agile method via:
  - an easy-to-use guide that explains the basics of Agile methods (such as the 'Agile Cookbook' that was created by BT)
  - formal education and certification courses for the selected method(s).
  - internal training sessions to walk through and demonstrate these methods.

Proper understanding of these principles and practices will significantly reduce the potential for the *misapplication* of Agile methods, which, if it occurs, could eliminate the possibility of wider organizational support altogether.

As the adoption of Agile methods grows and matures in your organization, you can further refine your use of Agile by enlisting qualified consultants, attending group training courses and reading industry resources, such as those listed in *More Information on Agile*.

One final thought: Every time staff members work on an Agile project, the organization is likely to grow more confident in these approaches. Management's initial gut reaction to resist empowering the team is replaced by the proven knowledge that this is an extremely effective way to achieve successful outcomes. Stakeholders' inclination to want everything delivered at once is replaced by an appreciation for prioritizing outputs by the business value that they can bring to the organization.

That is why it is so valuable for people who have been through the process before to assist the new areas in the organization who are trialling Agile methods. These experienced Agile resources can act as advisers and facilitators in the process, ensuring that practices are followed correctly, and allaying concerns that staff, managers or stakeholders might have as they move away from their traditional ways of working. Furthermore, once these areas have been through a couple of Agile initiatives, they can begin to take on the adviser role for others in the organization. This not only creates a larger (and stronger) network of Agile practitioners within the organization, it decentralizes the responsibility for any one area to be involved in each Agile initiative.

The bottom line is that your organization can achieve real productivity gains using Agile methods. The challenge is to implement Agile in a way that aligns with the specific needs, constraints and dynamics of your organization.

MORE INFORMATION ON AGILE

General information on Agile

Agile Alliance:
www.agilealliance.com

AgileCanberra Forum:
http://au.groups.yahoo.com/group/agilecanberra/

Agile Connection:
www.agileconnection.com

Agile Kiwi – Practical Agile Software Development:
www.agilekiwi.com

Agile Manifesto:
www.agilemanifesto.org

AgileSoftwareDevelopment.com:
www.agilesoftwaredevelopment.com

Alistair Cockburn:
http://alistair.cockburn.us/

Everything You Want to Know About Agile, Jamie Lynn Cooke, IT Governance Publishing (2012):
www.itgovernanceusa.com/shop/p-549-everything-youwant-to-know-about-Agile.aspx.

The Power of the Agile Business Analyst: 30 surprising ways a business analyst can add value to your Agile development team, Jamie Lynn Cooke, IT Governance Publishing (2013):
www.itgovernanceusa.com/shop/p-1379-the-power-of-the-agile-business-analyst.aspx

Specific Agile methods

Overview

A Practical Guide to Seven Agile methods:
www.devx.com/architect/Article/32761 (Part 1)
www.devx.com/architect/Article/32836 (Part 2)

Scrum

ScrumAlliance:
www.scrumalliance.org

Glossary of Scrum Terms, Szalvay V, Scrum Alliance, Inc. (2007):
www.scrumalliance.org/community/articles/2007/march/glossary-of-scrum-terms

Scrum and Agile Presentations by Mike Cohn of Mountain Goat Software, Cohn M (various dates):
www.mountaingoatsoftware.com/presentations

DSDM

What is DSDM?
www.codeproject.com/KB/architecture/dsdm.aspx

DSDM Explained:
www.agilexp.com/presentations/DSDMexplained.pdf

FDD™

Feature-Driven Development: An Overview
www.tarrani.net/mike/docs/fddoverview.pdf

Feature Driven Development (FDD) and Agile Modelling
www.agilemodeling.com/essays/fdd.htm

Lean

Lean Primer, Larman C & Vodde B (2009): *www.leanprimer.com/downloads/lean_primer.pdf*

Leading Lean Software Development: Results Are Not the Point:
www.poppendieck.com/pdfs/LLSD_intro.pdf

XP™

Extreme Programming: a gentle introduction:
www.extremeprogramming.org

RUP®

What is the Rational Unified Process®?:
www.ibm.com/developerworks/rational/library/content/RationalEdge/jan01/WhatIstheRationalUnifiedProcessJan01.pdf

Agile Modelling and the Rational Unified Process (RUP):
www.agilemodeling.com/essays/agileModelingRUP.htm

AUP

The Agile Unified Process (AUP):
www.ambysoft.com/unifiedprocess/agileUP.html

Kanban

Kanban (overview)
www.crisp.se/kanban

Scrumban

Scrum-ban: *http://leansoftwareengineering.com/ksse/scrum-ban/*

Scrumban - Essays on Kanban Systems for Lean Software Development, Ladas C, Modus Cooperandi Press (2009)

Kanban and Scrum – making the most of both, Kniberg H and Skarin M (2010):
www.infoq.com/minibooks/kanban-scrum-minibook

Scrumban: Taking Scrum Outside Its Comfort Zone
www.slideshare.net/yyeret/scrumban-taking-scrum-outside-its-comfort-zone

Scaled Agile Framework® (SAFe®)

Scaled Agile Framework® (SAFe®):
www.scaledagileframework.com

Introducing the Scaled Agile Framework®
www.cio.com/article/2936942/enterprise-software/introducing-the-scaled-agile-framework.html

Large-Scale Scrum (LeSS) Framework

Introduction to LeSS
http://less.works/less/framework/introduction.html

Nexus

Nexus Framework
www.scrum.org/Resources/The-Nexus-Guide

Scrum of Scrums

Agile Can Scale: Inventing and Reinventing SCRUM in Five Companies
www.controlchaos.com/storage/scrum-articles/Sutherland%20200111%20proof.pdf

Disciplined Agile Delivery (DAD)

The Disciplined Agile Framework
www.disciplinedagiledelivery.com/agility-at-scale/disciplined-agile-2/

Crystal

Crystal methods
http://alistair.cockburn.us/Crystal+methodologies

Industry research on Agile

9th Annual State of Agile Development Survey, VersionOne: *http://info.versionone.com/state-of-agile-development-survey-ninth.html*

The state of application development in enterprises and SMBs: business data services North America and Europe, Stone J, *Database and Network Journal* (1 April 2007): *www.thefreelibrary.com/The+state+of+application+development+in+enterprises+and+SMBs:...-a0162832944*

Selected Agile case studies

Agile Coaching in British Telecom, Meadows L & Hanly S (2006):
www.agilejournal.com/articles/columns/column-articles/144-agile-coaching-in-british-telecom

Rolling out Agile in a Large Enterprise, Benefield G, *Proceedings of the 41st Annual Hawaii International Conference on System Sciences (HICSS) (2008)*: *www.computer.org/portal/web/csdl/doi/10.1109/HICSS.2008.382*

Information on TQM and Kaizen

TQM. Total Quality Management. An Integrated Approach to Quality and Continuous Improvement, Kotelnikov V (last updated January 27, 2011)
www.1000ventures.com/business_guide/im_tqm_main.html

KAIZEN – The Japanese Strategy for Continuous Improvement, Kotelnikov V (last updated November 09, 2010): *www.1000ventures.com/business_guide/mgmt_kaizen_main.html*

Information on Lean manufacturing

Common Questions Organizations Ask About Lean Manufacturing, Keberdle CF, Lean Solutions Group, LLC (2008):
www.leansolutionsgroup.com/images/Common_Questions_About_Lean_Mfg.pdf

Lean Principles, Kilpatrick J, Utah Manufacturing Extension Partnership (2003):
http://www.inmatech.nl/res/pdfs/leanprinciples.pdf

ITG RESOURCES

IT Governance Ltd sources, creates and delivers products and services to meet the real-world, evolving IT governance needs of today's organisations, directors, managers and practitioners.

The ITG website (*www.itgovernance.co.uk*) is the international one-stop-shop for corporate and IT governance information, advice, guidance, books, tools, training and consultancy. On the website you will find the following page related to the subject matter of this book:

www.itgovernance.co.uk/project_governance.aspx.

Publishing Services

IT Governance Publishing (ITGP) is the world's leading IT-GRC publishing imprint that is wholly owned by IT Governance Ltd.

With books and tools covering all IT governance, risk and compliance frameworks, we are the publisher of choice for authors and distributors alike, producing unique and practical publications of the highest quality, in the latest formats available, which readers will find invaluable.

www.itgovernancepublishing.co.uk is the website dedicated to ITGP. Other titles published by ITGP that may be of interest include:

- The Power of the Agile Business Analyst

  www.itgovernance.co.uk/shop/p-1457.aspx

- Everything you want to know about Agile

  www.itgovernance.co.uk/shop/p-549.aspx

- Directing the Agile Organisation

  www.itgovernance.co.uk/shop/p-1369.aspx

We also offer a range of off-the-shelf toolkits that give comprehensive, customisable documents to help users create the specific documentation they need to properly implement a management system or standard. Written by experienced practitioners and based on the latest best practice, ITGP toolkits can save months of work for organisations working towards compliance with a given standard.

Please visit *www.itgovernance.co.uk/shop/c-129-toolkits.aspx* to see our full range of toolkits.

Books and tools published by IT Governance Publishing (ITGP) are available from all business booksellers and the following websites:

www.itgovernance.eu *www.itgovernanceusa.com*

www.itgovernance.in *www.itgovernancesa.co.za*

www.itgovernance.asia.

Training Services

IT Governance offers an extensive portfolio of training courses designed to educate information security, IT governance, risk management and compliance professionals. Our classroom and online training programmes will help you develop the skills required to deliver best practice and compliance to your organisation. They will also enhance your career by providing you with industry standard certifications and increased peer recognition. Our range of courses offer a structured learning path from Foundation to Advanced level in the key topics of information security, IT governance, business continuity and service management.

Full details of all IT Governance training courses can be found at

www.itgovernance.co.uk/training.aspx.

Professional Services and Consultancy

The IT Governance Professional Services team can show you how to apply Agile concepts to the most complex development projects. Our expert consultants can guide and inspire you in the use of Agile, providing you with the practical techniques to improve delivery efficiencies, control your implementation costs, and meet your sales targets by building customer loyalty.

We will show you the Agile methods that create flexibility and ensure adaptability to changing circumstances, accepting that nothing changes more than your customer's needs. You will learn how to change from a traditional hierarchy towards self-empowered individuals and teams. In this way, you will develop engaged employees with the responsibility, accountability and authority to deliver to the customer's requirements, shaping and directing outcomes, while regularly delivering partial, though functional, products.

For more information about IT Governance: Consultancy and Training Services see:

www.itgovernance.co.uk/consulting.aspx.

Newsletter

You can stay up to date with the latest developments across the whole spectrum of IT governance subject matter, including risk management, information security, ITIL and IT service management, project governance, compliance and so much more, by subscribing to our newsletter.

Simply visit our subscription centre and select your preferences:

www.itgovernance.co.uk/newsletter.aspx.

EU for product safety is Stephen Evans, The Mill Enterprise Hub, Stagreenan, Drogheda, Co. Louth, A92 CD3D, Ireland. (servicecentre@itgovernance.eu)

www.ingramcontent.com/pod-product-compliance
Lightning Source LLC
LaVergne TN
LVHW020652100826
845148LV00012B/2445